THE BEHAVIOR OF WORDS

THE BEHAVIOR OF WORDS

Efe Duyan

Translated by Aron Aji

WHITE PINE PRESS / BUFFALO, NEW YORK

White Pine Press
P.O. Box 236
Buffalo, NY 14201
www.whitepine.org

Publication of this book was supported by public funds from the New York State Council on the Arts, with the support of Governor Kathy Hochul and the New York State Legislature, a State Agency.

Acknowledgements:
Some of these translations have been previously published in the *Harvard Review, Poetry London,* and *Interpret.*

Cover Image: Elaine LaMattina

Printed and bound in the United States of America.

ISBN 978-1-945680-63-2

Library of Congress Control Number: 2022940639

THE BEHAVIOR OF WORDS

Contents

Translator's Note | 9

The Behavior of Words | 13
Coalescence | 15
First the Verbs Are Forgotten | 16
If Only | 17
Types of Dreams | 19
Hope | 21
Types of Happiness | 23
Shifting Shapes | 24
Creation | 26
Philosophical Theses on Love | 27
Transparent Words | 29
Maybe Except for Other Women | 30
I to You | 31
Future | 33
Along with Everything that Follows | 34
Rain | 35
Wind | 36
EKG | 37
Not Me | 38
Michaelangelo's Rock | 39
Present Time | 40
Garden Care | 41
First Law of Thermodynamics | 42
Solaris | 43
The Structure of The Eye | 44
Dermis | 45
To Each Other | 46
Between Us | 49
To You a Bit More Every Day | 51
Kirilove | 53
Morning Echo | 54
The Meaning of Spaces | 55

Morning Mythology | 56
Call Center | 58
Looking at You | 59
Ink | 60
Away from the World | 61
Rebirth | 62
Advice | 63
The Maggot Who Yields to the Worm | 64
Beautiful Things First | 65
Geese, Lizards, Elephants and The Dead | 66
The Nature of Our Relationship | 67
Memory | 68
As If | 69
Maybe One Day | 71
An Ant at Full Speed | 73
A Walnut Tree | 74
My Conscience Is a Hungry Fox | 76
Sweet-Tempered Anger | 77
Engin Çeber's Soon to Be Forgotten Death | 78
Death Effigy | 80
Slowly Receding | 82
The Worker Who Comes Across His Son
                in The Barricade of Soldiers | 83
Mehmet and Osman, Cevizli Cigarette Factory | 84

The Author | 85
The Translator | 87
Notes on the Poems | 88

Translator's Note

Some poems, built like houses with architectural intention, draw us in through their overall design, clean fine lines breaking at striking angles, guiding our eyes through carefully defined spaces opening to hallways that irresistibly lead us to unexpected enclosures where natural light plays among the walls breathe life into the lives for which they are intended. Where form and function are inseparable, the space is not merely for dwelling. It asks to be experienced. Physically, materially.

This is how I first experienced the work of Efe Duyan the Turkish poet who is also, unsurprisingly, a scholar of architectural history at Mimar Sinan University, named after the greatest Ottoman architect whose breathtaking structures lend Istanbul an unrivaled beauty.

Efe Duyan's verses are composed so patiently, meticulously that they may as well have been drawn rather than written. The lean interlacing of the words, the considered sparseness of the stanzas, the slow accretion of meaning along these afford the reader a striking transparency: we almost feel as if experiencing the poems taking shape as we read them.

These translations began during Efe Duyan's residency in the International Writing Program, at the University of Iowa, when I helped revise some of his draft translations. My principal aim was to strip the English text to its leanest and foreground as optimally as possible the formal ingenuity of both verse and poem. I remained true to the same aim when translating the rest of the poems that appear in this volume. Given the infamous incommensurabiltity of English and Turkish grammars, the process often required forcing the natural Turkish syntax, especially in Duyan's idiosyncratic manipulations, on the English in order to foreground the physical direction of the verse and the gradual accretion of meaning. In the Turkish originals, individual verses bring the reader to surprising semantic shifts and reversals; the movement through the poem, too, deftly builds on these surprise turns. As a native reader of Turkish, I wanted to concentrate especially on recreating their formal elegance, their seemingly effortless flow in the Turkish. At best, I tried to create poetry written in English inside intrinsically Turkish forms, resonant with sounds and shades of the original language.

— Aron Aji

THE BEHAVIOR OF WORDS

The Behavior of Words

every word that leaves my lips
shifts from shape to shape

like two hedgehogs
they copulate in the air
at times
the words turn into ice
and fall on the ground

mixed among the clouds
they become meaningless
at times
like kittens
they even refuse being loved

they feed on carnation petals
thrown at demonstrations
at times
they surrender to the wind
along with the pollens

like pigeons
they trust too easily
and not just at times
whenever I glance at you
they contest my glances

they may shift from shape to shape
but only
care for each other
the words
don't even notice us

they are the small egrets
perched on a cow's back
they don't care a whit about the world
or know that they change
the world

the words bind us together
like the quietude
of a river unaware
that it binds mountains
to the sea

Coalescence

soon everything will end
while we wait
we give each other new names

they know their sounds
but not their meanings

they jump like little children
over the fences encircling our minds
and scamper toward us

they must have grown thirsty
we drag all of them to the river with us
disguised as deer like the Olympian gods

if we reveal their meanings to them
they will burn
like meteors entering the atmosphere

and since we are gods
roaming the world
in our new names
we don't need to make wishes

we don't need their consolation
running short on time
we release the words into the river
with loving care

we release ourselves
to drink water from each other's mouth
greedily greedily

First the Verbs Are Forgotten

first the verbs are forgotten
breaking loose, they leave
each making
a small wave

next
the adjectives
we use attentively
to describe great sorrows
untranslatable into any language

next
the adverbs passed down
from a very old language
long extinct

next
the absurd exclamations
of our childhood
that had made us inexplicably happy

next the nouns grow dark
slow down
and flow with the rainwater
into the sea

only the fear of death remains

we no longer speak
but it keeps going like a pulse
to call the words back
nestled right here inside us waiting
for that nameless skill

If Only

If only: like a Swiss army knife
the heaven and hell we carry with us

If only: thanks to proverbs and special effects
our malice that we liken to compassion

If only: the inertia besieging all good ideas
soaking it in detergent water

If only: our good intentions
with a pair of steel pliers

If only: like women the lonely nights too
their inescapable disquiet

If only: the disasters born of lovelorn hearts
in the neat framework of logic

If only: the ruined walls of pagan temples
we encounter while making love

If only: a cheap gift with nicked corners
our childhood

If only: the bruising consolation of if onlys
through concrete examples

If only: all the lives
at once

If only: the great troubles
without waiting for a great revolution

If only: all the deaths
experienced one by one and personally

If only: the absence of meaning itself
with a razor blade

If only

Types Of Dreams

their packaging seldom lists the ingredients
and usually no expiration date

our selfishness doesn't bother them
like natural events, they are indifferent to us.

like animals, they can't, or won't
tell apart good from bad
and like trees, sometimes they don't bear fruit

some might be mistaken for miniature crematoria
some may require dexterity like using a scalpel
some can be doctored like an official document

some dreams stay in drawers
even knowing that comforts us
though others are like machines
if unused, they get old quickly

you inhabit some dreams
but just as you inhabit the universe
and still can't understand the universe
you can't understand those dreams either

some dreams make you a believer
but you can't prove that god exist
just as you can't prove the opposite

some are like polytheistic deities
they freely mingle among their worshippers

some
die slowly while coming true
some kill their owner if he gives up on them too soon

some readily include an operator's manual
to change the world
some have an arrest warrant against them

after all, different types of dreams—
like your birthplace and the city you love—
should be introduced to each other

like choppy waters and long journeys—
they should be enjoyed together

like love with sex—
mixed in the correct ratio

Hope

is a rough-cut key

a salad, wrapped in aluminum foil, never touched
and still fresh

it's defenseless against malware

a missed opportunity but will return someday

it's a booze-head's sincere confessions

a cartoon superhero
who, racing in the air, never falls
who knows how to win hearts
and, of course, never dies

it's an eraser
because all the borders
are first drawn on a map
in pencil

a flower left on a grave

it dries on the hair of a Libyan refugee drowned in the Mediterranean

glows in the eyes of a Japanese google-searching cancer
in the aftermath of a radiation leak

it flows dark and red in public squares in Ukraine

burns in the chest of a black boy in America

trembles in the hands of a Syrian woman looking at her wedding photo
among the ruins of her house

it quivers on the press-release Berkin's father holds in his hand

beats the shores, rolls in the mud, fancies a tern

and laughs stubbornly
somehow, we also laugh

Types Of Happiness

at times cheating in an exam is
happiness

at times a genetically modified dream
forgotten in the morning

at times it is lighting a cigarette to decompress
at times trying to quit smoking for good

it is fearing death
or while remembering your friends who died
it is rejoicing in those who will outlive you

at times
at times is happiness

happiness makes you believe you can change
happiness is at times like unhappiness
and maybe happiness is what you're living now
happiness   is good

Shifting Shapes

the sea is a stained tablecloth
you forget that each sea is also a lethal desert
and sit at the head of the table

you wonder whether
the desert
can really take the color of the sea
like a sky under your feet

actually everything assumes
each other's color

like a cactus needle
and its root
our shape-shifting emotions
are enjoined

you and I
will we really fall in love
I ask

your color diffuses
I dip my fingers in the water

you take off your clothes
unconcerned
and start swimming
in time's translucent sands

time
turns into a large newly painted room
with sofas and lampshades

right away we start
shifting the furniture around
as if changing the world unconcerned
that we're splashing the hardwood floor

Creation

I knew that even light would not escape a blackhole
because of the colossal gravitational field
when I saw you waiting for me outside the airport gate
I believed in god's existence
and that astronomy is a joke he tells us about fate
to win our sympathy

when I hugged you while cabdrivers circled around us
you turned into a black hole made of heart muscles
and responded, your pulse racing
to my questions about
your haircut
the time spent without me and
about creation

entering the house, you already knew I'd crossed the event horizon
you commanded *let there be compassion*, and there was compassion
and when you saw that compassion was good and separated it from pleasure
you saw that pleasure was good, and you commanded *let there be sweat*
and when you saw that sweat was good and you commanded
let rivers flow through our bodies
the first sound that came out of your mouth
was the big bang
of the universe
being created anew
in the void inside you

Philosophical Theses On Love

everything started around a beat-up table in NO
as if giving away a secret,
according to Schopenhauer, I thought back then
only the reproductive urge draws people together
yet love is etched in my mind like a tattoo
as a sketch drawn on a napkin
the finer details yet to be determined
love is an idea
a choice
we give secrets in shiny gift packages
we ride the air bubbles rising in the water
eager to reach the surface
before popping

it's dangerous
Sartre says
worse still for him, attachment inhibits freedom
I had noticed when we held hands
at a certain angle
our hands
perfectly fit together
your wrist-bone in my palm's hollow
my fingers wrapped around your fist-bones
I call it the angle of freedom
like that perfect angle
caught by an upwind sail

if you listen to Wittgenstein
you can love someone only as much as you can express it
I have no objection
because in that huge, even rather ugly park called Hickory
where nouns, breaking off the objects they signify
fell to the world
like rain drops
and our love suddenly rekindled itself
hurry, we said, *we have little time*
*let us also go to where language end*s
carrying in our bags rich, creamy beginnings
spread on sandwich bread
we reclined on camping chairs
and watched love's clouds relieved of secrets
till the names reevaporated

Transparent Words

we had our different countries, our different relationships
when our plane experienced turbulence
the words we taught each other to calm ourselves
became seahorses
twisting their tails together
in deep ocean currents
because they could not swim otherwise

Maybe Except for Other Women

after a deep breath
hanging up the phone
crisscrossing the continents
our proud silence
is a wild animal

it will never be tamed

holding its breath
as if pouncing upon a bird
it will pounce upon
everything crossing my mind
that is not you

I   to You

I   faraway to you? not really
a bus plus a ferry plus a tram

I   forbidden to you, let's not exaggerate
I look into your eyes and see
the other end of a freshly dug tunnel

I   a child to you, so be it
I love being spoiled beside you

I   anxious to you, I know
I sometimes exaggerate, dear tutor

I   inclined to you, don't ever move
as when one wave merges with the other wave

I   both the morning and the evening to you
the cunning fox of indecision

I   maudlin to you
we didn't meet too late, did we?

I   maybe a bother to you
will you be able to start over?

I   a blank sheet of paper to you
and the wood scent of the recently sharpened pencil

I   now to you
the eager hum of a watch just back from repair

I   then to you, always to you, you to you

I   let's to you
you're sure, aren't you?

I
a simple question asked to you

Future

I sit next to you on the deck
we try not to mention the past
a wind-swollen sail
can pull the boat any which way
except
windward

Along With Everything That Follows

neither an inflected form in a sentence
nor meaningful by itself
but altering
ad infinitum
everything that precedes
a conjunction
is the day we first met

Rain

we go to the oak forests often
easily bored at home
your home, sorry, our home, is tiny
I know if they grow too close to each other
oak trees won't thrive
still, on cloudless nights
we won't sleep unless in each other's arms

Wind

I rub my finger
and taste the dust
gathered on the table

the wind
first rubbed itself against
a stray dog's wet nose

it shook
the leaves on an apricot tree

lingered
on my beloved's hair while she worked

swept the newspapers off
the bodies lying on the ground after a crash

now I smell

pollen
saliva
sweat
and blood

the wind whooshes our love
like an orange plastic bag

EKG

you arrived early
I hang my wet towel on the chair
your ekg on the table

no two heartbeats
are ever alike
like fingerprints
matchless

if i don't know you better than anyone else
can i truly love

i'm looking for traces
that only belong to you

along the zigzags of the red graph paper
suddenly
the horizon line of an island
covered with hills

Not Me

as soon as I kiss you
an ice floe
enters my veins
and while melting slowly
it circulates through my body

I hold my breath
the world stops
and I feel like a diviner
in the darkness of space
constellations come alive
the great bear's tail, the lion's eye
the memories of extinguished stars
fall on the crumpled sheets
we look like an artist's palette

color names
roll off my tongue
in a language long erased from the earth

I lean and kiss you again
this time
everything I've known
flows across my body
and down
the drain of the universe

I know
only my body will remember we made love
not me

Michaelangelo's Rock

inside every rock
a statue

another world
in this world's future

you
(even if I don't notice)
an organ
slowly growing inside me

Present Time

right before seeing in some corner
a disemboweled ginger tabby
we had been petting street cats lovingly

once you see the bowels
nothing will look the same

I decide to resist
tinkering with our past

Garden Care

we're in the summer place
some flowers, hiding during the day
open at night
we keep our nights long
tending to our relationship along with the garden
at times with sweet praise, with saliva at others
long, long hours, talking through everything
then at times
hiding
what we truly think

First Law Of Thermodynamics

it's starting to rain
a saki reaching for rakı

cuddled in the middle of the bed
we assume the shape of a drop

according to Sun Simiao, the alchemist,
mercury, sulfur and arsenic mixed together
can yield pure liquids and ideal
geometric shapes
we wish each other goodnight
and dive into wet snail dreams

while Nicolas Flamel, the parisian notary,
claimed to have created gold in thirteen eighty-two
our blanket turns into a hard and lustrous shell
in this way we change shapes
tortoises live very long
they enjoy anise leaves

about good tavern manners
or which river the rainwater flows to around here? we wonder
we look up the first law of thermodynamics in a book

the world was born before us
we will die
the tortoises will die
the anise leaves will rot
the shapes, my dear
will preserve
our love

for when the rivers die
they become seas

Solaris

ashes
swirl in the wind and cling to our clothes
I join together our shared moments
so that a film reel made of frames
comes alive on the sand-shore
no one wants to take the empty urn
the fresh meat of a bloodied animal

memories are born out of the corpses
of moments
the sun glows
the taste of the frigid north wind
I'm reminded of *Solaris*

even if memories don't come back to life
they change
and when their traces disappear
is this when someone truly dies
or begins to live
his own life instead

we stop by a kiosk on the way back
the souls we thought were dead
remember us
in their borrowed memory

tell them, no meat in my soup, I say to you
I've yet to learn your native language

the trace we leave in each other's life
a wet sand-shore
as the wave disappears

The Structure of the Eye

my eyes
give names
to your birthmarks
like the ancient astronomers
by looking at their shapes

before each discoloration
along your limbs
they bow in reverence

their eyelashes imbibe
the sweat off your back
trying to replenish the eye white

and diving
beneath your cornea
my eyes want to swim
among the light beams
seeping through

and to record everything you see
to project it on a screen
they hang on the wall

and going deeper
they want
to kiss you
on your blind spot

Dermis

our skin
makes up 16% of our body weight
I spread your skin under me
a white sheet
tightening
as it wraps itself around me
a melancholy seagull
with wide open wings

our skin actually
renews itself entirely every month
my fingers comb through your hair
loose specks of dried skin catch my hand
the ruckus of spring insects
mixes with your pulsation
the ivy along your veins grows
my eyes are closed
you whisper, *wait until*
you see the green around here

your skin turns
into a curly rain cloud
my eyes part
we are newborns, soaking wet

the seagull releases a shriek
looking around to see if anyone has heard it
its wings scraping river's skin

To Each Other

with fisherman's knots that actually
      come undone when the right end is pulled
with transmissible microbes perhaps

at times on an out-of-tune piano
      allegro ma non troppo
at times from the edge of a precipice
      down to to bottom at maximum speed

without moving too far from our neighborhood
      on the colorful clotheslines that smell of detergent
like the continents drifting unnoticed
      traveling each year only small distances

with the collar button of a black school uniform
      look since how long
like two snakes shedding their skins
      each new season

curiously in the darkness
      of an ocean floor
like morning coffee
      and also out of habit

sealed tight with the superglue
      that leaks onto your fingertips
or is it with the serenity
      of a Sunday morning

with the aluminum foil the street-corner gypsy
      wraps the lilacs in on special days
with an IV line
      in cases of emergency

with the modest movements
     of hydrogen and oxygen atoms
while startled at the possibility of life
     in a newly discovered planet

with the identical plates
     of a scale
but without caring that we want
     no balance whatsoever

with the horns of absolutely
      untamable animals
during the sleep cycle
      of the noisy cicadas

with the the squirrel's scent
      that the fox follows
and the fox's footsteps
      that the squirrel hears

confusing the fear
     that a bomb can explode anytime
with the worry that we may run out
     of milk for coffee

like a tombstone
and the person who gently washes the tombstone
come what may

while some revolution turns into a counterrevolution
maybe because we are watching it together

economizing our convictions
to not die of thirst

wary of
commitment

with the sound
of my skin rubbing against your skin

by drying in the sun
the lactic acid collecting in our patience

with the puppet strings
we hold in our own hands

to each other
you and I

Between Us

when brewed and ingested
the thirsty leaves of the juniper we planted
cause temporary blindness

between us
the roots of two olive trees
twist and twine under the blanket

between us
a breath's span
closing fast

between us
the iodine smell mixed with cement dust
tugging at our hands

between us
a Sunday laziness
retuning the rest of the days

between us
two glasses of ouzo
iced white

between us
a time that belongs to us
falls off laughing sometimes

between us
like an ill-timed song
that silence
starts without warning

the emptiness between us
stirs us both awake near daybreak

the emptiness between us
learns everything between us
at uncommon speed

To You a Bit More Every Day

because of the indistinct
burn scar
a gas bomb left on my hand
some years ago

unworried
despite the sound of a blast
that's been lodged in our ears
for months

while dreaming of swimming
this morning in the mass grave
that the Mediterranean has become

unhurried
even at this very moment

using just in case
the bellows of an accordion
to enjoin our memories

in the sudden rain
in the quiet of milk
suffusing the coffee
Be careful, it's hot!

undoubting
like the water drops
that will return to the atmosphere

like the roots
of olive trees
sometimes from miles away

while keeping in mind
the eagle-owl
we can never seem to spot
who switches its diet not its nest
when the hunt is low

because we don't leave the table
before eating every last morsel
to honor a dead animal

and because
no part of you
I've left unpraised
as deserved

Kirilove

sweetlovska I call you
didn't we learn love from the Russian novels

the first evening you laid next to me
etched in my memory in cuneiform
no, no: a cave drawing

in the beginning I'd made you wait a bit
forgive me for that much

for a while I kept your name secret
you don't know why

the scarf you were knitting half-finished
so be it, winter will come again
and your half solitude, still lovely

on my way out in the morning, you had handed me an apple
let it be our password

and let your eyebrows grow
artificiality frightens me
in some architecture, even in poetry

your legs are covered with childhood scars
the quickstep of our lovemaking
our love patient like your hair growing

but I still confuse the long nicknames
in those Russian novels

Morning Echo

off the petals
the indecisive oleander
lifts near sunrise

off the wind-thirsty wings
of a seagull
readying for the hunt

off the babbling rainwater
wandering the street gutters
asking for directions

off the empty bench facing the sea,
the salty wood cracking a bit more
each passing day

off the belated, two-short-
one-long whistle
of the Karaköy ferry

off the applause opening
a protest rally

bounces and returns
the sigh you held in your mouth
awhile longer
after lovemaking

The Meaning of Spaces

it's the spaces in-between
that connect the words,
not the conjunctions

it's the distance that connects
person A to person B, not the speed
at which they run to each other

it's A's honesty toward B that divides
our life into small swallowable morsels

that A is nothing like B is maybe
what in practice preserves our balance

that A is sometimes angry with B
is what sets the dialectics
of our peaceful home lives

or it is a question B asks A
that A suddenly finds during an argument
like a long-lost object

it is a survival technique B uses
that A will justify one day

what connects A and B
is not the conjunctions
but the absence itself

in other words: the space between us
is like the great revolutions
everything they touch is transformed

Morning Mythology

the gods were still asleep
my joy of living
was feeding on
my fear of death

dust had gathered
on the dreams I told you about

I'd been steering my youth
like pushing a shopping cart
slowpoke, hipshot

*

the gods had not yet started
their daily chores

the dreams I didn't tell you about
I was making into gifts and souvenirs

my morning cheer
was feeding not on people
but, strangely, on my fears

*

the gods were still yawning
the worlds they'd made, some already worn out
I turned to you, wearing away
but not turning into you

at the end of every dream
the ants returning from a wedding
waved white towels at us

and when I woke up
my power over what I had seen—
poof— would suddenly disappear

I loved you
but was feeding on
the loneliness of others

    *

I don't blame you
for anything

we haven't taken a long trip yet this summer
I'm starting to forget my dreams quickly

the gods
have planted their jaws at road ends
they drink our sweat at breakfast
strangely, not our blood

Call Center

welcome
to relive the day you met your school friends
please press your lucky number
for the times you ran tirelessly around the yard
press random numbers
for the steamed-up windows of truck stops
enter the year of your last family summer vacation

everybody has times they're ashamed of
pick a number and keep it to yourself
for the tea and *poğaça* breakfasts on the campus green
put the receiver down and run to the balcony
if you wish to complain about time rushing helter-skelter
please press and hold zero with all your strength
if you can't quite remember your grandfather
look in the mirror

for the dust smell in vintage bookstores
say the third letter of the name
of a laborer who can't read or write
for your neighborhood tailor who was found dead in tattered clothes
please hold

for the woman in your sleep
for that unforeseen moment when you touched her neck
wait for the beep then
press the same number over and over

the day after you were ditched
write in your notebook one hundred times
I will never fall in love again

beep

Looking At You

Upturning the turtle, little girl runs away
For the first time, turtle sees sky

Ink

once it got under my skin
I can't get rid of it

without tearing off
a piece of my skin

like your presence

now

your absence too

Away from the World

without a certain distance
you can't fully grasp anything
this distance soon turns into an untouched valley
with a river flowing through
a bee flies down and washes its face

a bit of happiness
depends on forgetting distances
what you've forgotten
like a tree bearing green apples
that fall in the river
whenever you lean down to drink
you grow thirstier

if asked as a child you would've said
all the decisions you'll make
are the mouthfuls of bites
you take out of an apple

Rebirth

my soul was not in this world for some time
then I was born
and rebirth
stayed with me as a bad habit

Advice

ankle-deep in my dream
the wind speaks
rock faces change
as does the face of death, she says
better use your face as a mask
don't forget
the sea also speaks
I caress her
with the palm of my hand
then I scoop up the water
like digging a grave
to understand yourself
you must understand the other, he says
I don't know who the other is

then the sun speaks
we can't see it rising
or setting from our house
only a voice
love
is the symbol, it says
of whatever you want
self-confident
be strong and tend to your symbols

The Maggot Who Yields to the Worm

we are in the summer house
a new planet is discovered
the thorns on the rose trees glisten
actually it's an ordinary evening
we are looking at the sky
time's tides cascade over our bodies

we are in Sarayburnu, looking at the pile
of rubble left of the tea garden
that collapsed as soon as we left
while the wound of the universe
scabs over by and by

we are on a volcanic Greek island
magma is just about to touch the atmosphere
we are anxiously looking like everyone else
at the sulfurous earth
the universe is stitching itself
it will have a scar

we are in the cemetery
the weather is still hot
a blind maggot is yielding to a blind worm
through the tear on a grave-cloth
we are holding hands
looking at each other
maybe the universe is fine the way it is
maybe it doesn't need to heal

Beautiful Things First

we're in the kitchen
your back is turned to me
in our mouths the sour taste
of spinach and missed opportunities
another day of our life has passed
but we're home, we're happy

you're brewing tea
your own blend
we can see inside the world now
it's beautiful without us
and self-possessed

we go out for a walk
as we walk quietly
what you scatter along the edges of our path
will grow one day

when we return I notice
the geraniums on the windowsill
can you believe, an entire year already

beautiful things are first to remind us
that we will die one day

Geese, Lizards, Elephants and the Dead

years go by
I stop to drink water
from the belly of newborn babies
it tastes like sour cherry juice

when tired, I wash my face
with the sweat
gathered at the creases

the geese fly
in V formation
the tired ones move
to the back of the line
catching their breaths
in the backdraft

time frightens all of us
a lizard abandons its tail
never ever returns
where it abandoned it

elephants
bury their dead
throwing soil over them
with their trunks

I bury in my memory
my dead ones each by each
I toss a cherry pit among them
and move to the end of the line

The Nature Of Our Relationship

the camera inside the nest
is broadcasting live to 3000 people
in this unfamiliar setting
I stay alive by feeding on
my emotions
frozen eaglets
food for the mother
so she gives birth again

Memory

the female velvet spider
that allows her babies
to eat her
when the time is right—
every beautiful thing
that happened to us

As If

as if our own gods
with the Play-Doh stored in the attic

as if indifference
is the devil's role
according to Lego building instructions

as if misery
as a prophet elect
to reflect the truth in its mirror

as if hope
to be sent down
as a great religion

as if the skies
with watercolors
for you and I to walk together under

as if the earth
a soccer turf in the evening
to relieve stress with high school friends

as if the water
to end the disputes about happiness
in a sailboat on the Mediterranean

as if the fire
to seep through the capillaries of rosewood pipes
and fill the room with cherry tobacco smell

as if everything we hold as truth
knowing that we will doubt them one day

as if our beliefs
to taste betrayal through them

as if the impossible
to falsify it with Galileo's formulas
by observing the movement of the stars

as if societies
to ask: *is art for art's sake or for society's sake?*
and to answer: *no, actually, society is for art's sake*

as if our faiths
from a light placenta-like material
that we can tear easily

as if the beauty of dissent
to wear proudly around our neck
so our life has a purpose

as if the present time
like a nine/eight gypsy tune

Maybe One Day

maybe
the stubborn habits
we pluck like loose buttons
in a fit of laughter

maybe
the unacknowledged grief
we share
like a birthday cake

maybe
fate
we slice finely with a large bread knife
and turn into an architectural whimsy

maybe
the absence of a departed we receive like a gift
and place in the most special corner
of the house

maybe
the fear of death
we throw in the bonfire
along with dry branches to add spark to our joy

maybe
everything lost to my memory
I blow into
a colorful balloon

maybe
all the words
into polysemous words
as acts of political dissent

maybe
the evil that the world serves in a picture-menu
after we confess we can't know everything
in the name of everyone

maybe
the seed of a hostile instinct
before it turns
into a massacre that we will read about in books

maybe
the plans to save the world
after asking the world
how it wants to be saved

maybe
seizing our own puppet strings
every incontestable taboo
zealously

maybe
no, absolutely
ourselves too

An Ant At Full Speed

the end of the world is near
the air crystal clear
the south wind against our face triggers migraine

sometimes our hopes come true
leaving long fracture marks on the shinbone

a dark blue pus burns through the sutures
a cat clawing from inside
asking you to open the window

like an effervescent tablet
before bedtime I drop in the water
all my opinions about revolutions
for some reason I love *Theses on Feuerbach*
and I fill the dreams I want to remember later
inside a water bottle

I observe closely
an ant running at full speed
and take notes
for the long speech
I plan to give
when the world ends
like the falcon
who glides awhile longer
after its heart has stopped

A Walnut Tree

actually I'd forgotten that
whenever I see a walnut tree
I remember again
two thousand seven or eight
when the police assaulted me
actually I'd felt shame

I remember
written on the police report that
we knocked down a special-op
kicked him and broke his nose
which I almost found laughable
I'd forgotten that

I remember
spending a week in a closed prison
crammed with a few robbers, smugglers
and a (real) murderer
I'd forgotten that

I remember
being unsure when I'd be released
certain
that my life was almost over
in a cell with six bunkbeds
and twenty people taking turns
sleeping
how I learned
the fine art of homemade tattoos
(their color later fading to leaf-green)
how I was amused watching
men jump excitedly at squirrels
darting across the courtyard wall
how I spent a week

crumpling little notes and flinging them
through the walnut branches
messaging the neighboring cell
and how I was wary
of inmates whose paths should never be crossed
crossing my path
I'd forgotten that

I remember
giving away my clothes when leaving
(because it's the custom)
and how everyone hugged me hurriedly
and with earnest cheer
I'd forgotten that

I remember
being slapped in the face right before leaving
for paying the prison director insufficient respect
and made to stand at attention
like an errant student
and thinking
if they detained me longer for this reason
that I would never forgive myself
for acting who I am
I'd forgotten that

I don't know which is better
to forget or to remember

I know
new trees grow only if
the squirrels forget where they bury
their walnuts

My Conscience Is A Hungry Fox

every night before bed

I crush the beggars' whispers
on a mortar

to sweeten
I add a pinch of the wind
whipping the faces of workers
fallen off the buildings

revolutionaries are painting banners
I take the goodness of their heart
onto a frying pan

I add the blood still warm
of a man stabbed in the street

I mix everything in a separate bowl
and set it outside my door

because my conscience is a hungry fox

but once he is full
he purrs like a cat
lying down next to me
we dive into dreams together

Sweet-Tempered Anger

like a well-read book
it fidgets inside my bag
wherever I go

at the first chance
it sheds its antlers like a reindeer
and runs away

the world is not to its liking
I understand

it's amazed how in the absence of justice
we can laugh and enjoy ourselves

to laugh is to resist, I explain
it considers asking your opinion, but is unsure

not never, sometimes it loses itself
that's when
it'll only listen to you
remember the statue inside the stone, you whisper

I think my anger, too, is a woman
she believes
she can give birth to beauty

Engin Çeber's Soon To Be Forgotten Death

I don't know him
a newspaper clipping out of millions
except for a passing glance
I don't know Engin Çeber
we put the same melancholy mask
on every dead man's face
or was he called Ergin? did his surname start with a "c" instead?
when has death become so commonplace
since when is "life" a familiar word
looked for in a foreign language?

who was Engin Çeber, we don't know
he was born, grew up, and the newspaper here
gives the details of his death due to torture
at the police headquarters

and I am certain he was afraid not of dying
but of his death being misunderstood
this loneliness is not Engin Çeber's
it is our loneliness

I would have liked to hear your last heartbeat
to touch the last object you saw, to know your last words
or when was the last time you smiled?
—your friends say you always smiled—
when did your hat fall off your head?
your head is bare in the photograph taken at the prison gate
—yet they say you never removed your hat—
and the last thing you thought of, old lovers perhaps?
did you worry about your father, forgetting yourself?
he'll be back on the eve of the feast—so says your father—
or did you imagine, *once I'm out of here?*
—*he was full of life*, they say about you—
But I don't know you, Engin, were you?

did you use to love life so much?

were it not so, the emptiness between
defiance and grief on a newspaper clipping
would not have saddened us so much
this emptiness that's left of your body, cold
despite the love, the red carnations
and the tens of hands carrying your coffin
would not have drawn us into itself

you were full of life, certainly
—we'd know as much even if they didn't say so—
soon I will take a hat from the closet
your hatless photograph is in front of me
I wonder if you used to wear something like mine?
you see, we still don't know you
you and Engin Çeber's
soon to be forgotten death

Death Effigy

it turns out Różewicz preoccupied as he was
with other urgent matters had forgotten
that he also needed to die

I pull my death effigy aside and ask
what those carnations signify
in Yaşar Kemal's autographed book
and which string Yunus Emre strummed
right when he said "souls will not submit to death"

kidding, just kidding
I know we are in Istanbul
I know in Istanbul
no one greets peacefully
death as holy transcendence
it is stuck on the blade of your boat's propeller
like a jellyfish
a knot cast into your memory follows you

no you don't grieve
for the thirty-some billion dead homosapiens
for one maybe
maybe for a few

that herb of immortality
if you only knew
its latin name
you'd have shaken off your mind
the letters that separate
don't forget from can't forget

I know *forhope* is not a word
I toss a few carnation seeds
into my mouth
and bang!
I shoot my effigy

Slowly Receding

every next second I see it as something else
this cloud
my father and I in a beer joint
the only afternoon
we had spent together

The Worker Who Comes Across His Son
In The Barricade Of Soldiers

my throat has dried
but it doesn't seem to become quiet

my throat is calloused
from carrying placards on silver trays

my throat is a scary rope-walker
it doesn't know that it is possible to stand on the rope
only by marching forward
in front of the barricade of soldiers

my throat is scared out of its wits
while soldiers' helmets
are waving by our wind

my throat is blind
isn't it my own son
hidden in a uniform
indicating me with his rifle

my throat is racing with my legs
blusters like children's gang
while leaping up over the barricade

with my throat spread wide
I hug my son

my throat is knotted
keeps the joy to itself

my throat is slit
the blood of five others
leaking asunder

Mehmet And Osman, Cevizli Cigarette Factory

Mehmet also has his anxious Mehmet
like when he became a father

and his shy Mehmet too
like when he got married

he also got himself a distrustful Mehmet
by necessity

all of his Mehmets got merrily along
next to him Osman too had many Osmans he didn't know

did he have another, a sacrificial Mehmet?
Mehmet doesn't know
he didn't have time to figure it out
when he saw the gun aimed at them

a police badge in his pocket, Osman's undercover Osman
held a tobacco worker's hand
for the first time in Mehmet's lifeless Mehmet
that's when Mehmet's willful Mehmet walked
all the way to Taksim Square
grieved by his wife's memories
tore up his last regrets
in Osman's resignation letter

it felt good to lock horns with death
even after death

Efe Duyan

Born in 1981 in Istanbul, Turkey, poet, translator, and architect Efe Duyan's published work in Turkish includes the poetry collections *Sıkça Sorulan Sorular* (*Frequently Asked Questions*, 2016), *Tek Şiirlik Aşklar* (*One Poem Stands*, 2012) and, *Takas* (*Swap*, 2006). *Poetry on the Street: Selected Poems* appeard in Chinese in Taiwan in 2021. His work has been included in the anthology of Turkish poetry *Paper Ship* (2013), the European poetry anthology *Grand Tour* (2019), and *Europoesie — 21st Century Poetry Anthology* (2019). He is the author of the critical essay, *The Construction of Characters in Nâzım Hikmet's Poetry* (2008) and editor of the contemporary poetry anthology, *Bir Benden Bir O'ndan* (*One from Me, One from Him*, 2010). His critical fantasy novel on empathy, *Başka* (*Other*), was released in 2022.

He has also translated and published poetry collections by Radu Vancu (Romania), Matthias Göritz (Germany), Lloyd Schwartz (USA), and Madara Gruntmane (Latvia)

His work has appeared in numerous international journals including *Modern Poetry in Translation*, *Poetry Wales*, *Plume Poetry Magazine*, *Turkish Poetry Today*, *Exchanges: Journal of Literary Translation*, *Manoa: A Pacific Journal of International Writing*, and *3 AM Online Poetry Magazine* in the US and the UK.

His poems have been translated into Bulgarian, Bosnian, Czech, Chinese, Croatian, Danish, Dutch, English, Estonian, French, Greek, German, Hebrew, Hungarian, Italian, Japanese, Kurdish, Latvian, Lithuanian, Macedonian, Maltese, Occitan, Polish, Romanian, Russian, Serbian, Slovenian, Slovakian, Spanish, Swedish, and Ukrainian.

He has participated in numerous international events including the

Edinburgh Book Festival, London Book Fair, Berlin Poetry Festival, Mexico City Poetry Festival, Sidi Bou Said Poetry Festival in Tunisia, and the Word Express project.

He has been a visiting poet-in-residence at the University of Iowa's International Writing Program and held a Hurst Visiting Professorship at St. Louis University in Missouri and has given guest lectures on poetry at Ca-Foscari University, Georgia State University, George Washington University, the University of Iowa, and St. Louis University, and was a short-term scholar at the University of Massachusett, Boston.

He is currently on the architecture and design faculty at Riseba University of Applied Sciences in Riga, Latvia.

Aron Aji

Aron Aji, Director of Translation programs at the University of Iowa, is a native of Turkey, and has translated works by modern and contemporary Turkish writers, including Bilge Karasu, Elif Shafak, Latife Tekin, Murathan Mungan, and Ferit Edgü. His Karasu translations include *Death in Troy, The Garden of Departed Cats,* (2004 National Translation Award); and *A Long Day's Evening,* (NEA Literature Fellowship; finalist, 2013 PEN Translation Prize). He and David Gramling (as co-translators) received the 2021 Global Humanities Translation Prize for Murathan Mungan's *Valor: Stories* (2022). Aji's most recent translation is *Ferit Edgü's Wounded Age and Eastern Tales* (2023).

Notes on the Poems

Page 22 - Berkin Elvan (1999 — 2014) was a fifteen-year-old boy who was killed by police brutality. He was hit on the head by a tear-gas canister fired by a police officer in Istanbul during the June 2013 anti-government protests in Turkey. He died on March 11, 2014.

Page 27- Arthur Schopenhauer, (1788–1860) was a German philosopher. Often called the "philosopher of pessimism," he was primarily important as the exponent of a metaphysical doctrine of the will. His writings influenced later existential philosophy and Freudian psychology.

Jean-Paul Sartre (1905 — 1980) was one of the key figures in the philosophy of existentialism, a French playwright, novelist, screenwriter, political activist, biographer, and literary critic, as well as a leading figure in 20th-century French philosophy and Marxism.

Page 28 - Ludwig Wittgenstein (1889 — 1951) was an Austrian-British philosopher who worked primarily in logic, the philosophy of mathematics, the philosophy of mind, and the philosophy of language. He is considered by some to be the greatest philosopher of the 20th century.

Page 42 - Sun Simiao was a Chinese physician and writer of the Sui and Tang dynasty. He was titled as China's King of Medicine for his significant contributions to Chinese medicine and tremendous care to his patients.

Nicolas Flamel (c. 1330 — 1418) was a French scribe and manuscript-seller. After his death, Flamel developed a reputation as an alchemist believed to have created and discovered the philosopher's stone and to have thereby achieved immortality.

Page 43 - *Solaris* is a 2002 sci-fi film based on the 1961 novel by Polish writer Stanislaw Lem.

Page 46 - *Allegro ma non troppo* is a tempo mark indicating that the passage is to be played *allegro* (brisk or lively) but not too much so.

Page 54 - The Karaköy ferry crosses the Bosphorus between Europe and Asia in Istanbul.

Page 56 - Poğaça is a savory Turkish pastry.

Page 64 - Sarayburnu is a promontory quarter separating the Golden Horn and the Sea of Marmara in Istanbul. The area, which is where Topkapı Palace and Gülhane Park are located, was added to the UNESCO World Heritage List in 1985.

Page 70 - Nine/eight is a time signature in music indicating that there are nine eighth-note beats per bar.

Page 71 - A polysemous word is a word having several meanings, such as "bank."

Page 73 - *Theses on Feuerbach*, written by Karl Marx and originally published in 1888, consists of eleven short, philosophiocal notes critical of Grtmsan philosopher Ludwig Feuerbach's argument that human beings must have created religion in an attempt to assert themselves against their natural limitations.

Page 78 - Engin Çeber (1979 – 2008) was a Turkish human rights activist who was tortured and killed while in police custody. In 2012, in what Amnesty International called a landmark case, twelve prison guards and officials received prison sentences in connection with his death.

Page 78 - Tadeusz Różewicz, (1921 – 2014) was a Polish poet and playwright, and one of the leading writers of the post-World War II period.

Yaşar Kemal (1923 – 2015) was a Turkish writer and human rights activist and one of Turkey's leading writers.

Yunus Emre (1238–1328) was a Turkish folk poet and Islamic Sufi mystic who greatly influenced Turkish culture.

Page 84 - Taksim Square, located in the new area on the European side of Istanbul, is a major tourist and leisure district.